T0005066

WEiRD WEATHER

Jackie Golusky

Lerner Publications ◆ Minneapolis

Copyright © 2024 by Lerner Publishing Group, Inc.

All rights reserved. International copyright secured. No part of this book may be reproduced, stored in a retrieval system, or transmitted in any form or by any means—electronic, mechanical, photocopying, recording, or otherwise—without the prior written permission of Lerner Publishing Group, Inc., except for the inclusion of brief quotations in an acknowledged review.

Lerner Publications Company
An imprint of Lerner Publishing Group, Inc.
241 First Avenue North
Minneapolis, MN 55401 USA

For reading levels and more information, look up this title at www.lernerbooks.com.

Main body text set in Aptifer Sans LT Pro.
Typeface provided by Linotype AG.

Editor: Brianna Kaiser **Designer:** Mary Ross **Photo Editor:** Annie Zheng

Library of Congress Cataloging-in-Publication Data

Names: Golusky, Jackie, 1996– author.
Title: Weird weather / Jackie Golusky.
Description: Minneapolis : Lerner Publications, [2024] | Series: Wonderfully weird (Alternator books) | Includes bibliographical references and index. | Audience: Ages 8–12 | Audience: Grades 4–6 | Summary: "Weather changes from day to day, but sometimes it may change in an odd or unbelievable way. Readers will love learning about the weird weather that can and does happen all around the world"— Provided by publisher.
Identifiers: LCCN 2022038326 (print) | LCCN 2022038327 (ebook) | ISBN 9781728490755 (lib. bdg.) | ISBN 9798765604144 (pbk.) | ISBN 9798765601990 (eb pdf)
Subjects: LCSH: Weather—Juvenile literature.
Classification: LCC QC981.3 .G68 2024 (print) | LCC QC981.3 (ebook) | DDC 551.5—dc23/eng20221209

LC record available at https://lccn.loc.gov/2022038326
LC ebook record available at https://lccn.loc.gov/2022038327

Manufactured in the United States of America
1-53006-51024-12/8/2022

TABLE OF CONTENTS

INTRODUCTION:

IT'S RAINING FISH?

DARK CLOUDS GATHER IN THE SKY. Rain begins to fall along with something else: fish! But how can it be raining fish? How did the fish get in the clouds?

Raining fish is rare. It happens when a waterspout (*pictured*), a windstorm that spins around in a funnel shape, travels over a large body of water such as a lake or ocean. Waterspouts form between clouds and water.

But sometimes waterspouts don't only pick up water. They can pick up animals in the water such as fish, frogs, and crabs. Waterspouts have even carried squid and alligators. A waterspout can carry the animals for miles as the storm moves.

Raining animals is only one type of weird weather. Plenty of other strange weather events occur.

CHAPTER 1:
WEIRDER TOGETHER

SOMETIMES TWO WEATHER EVENTS COME TOGETHER IN UNEXPECTED WAYS. The combined weather events can make conditions hot, cold, windy, or just plain strange.

VOLCANIC LIGHTNING

When a volcanic eruption and lightning combine, volcanic lightning (*pictured*) occurs! Typically, lightning happens in a thundercloud when ice crystals combine and become electrically charged. Volcanic lightning happens in the volcano's smoke but without the thundercloud. It happens either high up in the volcano's smoke or close to the ground.

When ice forms high up in volcanic smoke, lightning forms in the usual way. How volcanic lightning forms closer to the ground is a little weirder. The volcano's ash rubs together and creates static electricity. This keeps happening until enough static electricity exists to create a lightning bolt.

SHOCKING!

If you rub your feet on a carpet and then shock someone, you make static electricity. It happens when the surface of an object has an electrical charge. Rubbing your feet on the carpet is similar to the volcano's ash rubbing together. Instead of making a shock, the ash makes a lightning bolt.

Waterspouts (*shown here*) and snowspouts both happen when rotating columns of air travel over water.

SNOWSPOUT

A snowspout is similar to a waterspout. It's often called a winter waterspout. This rotating column of air travels over water. But since the temperature is below freezing, the water isn't liquid. It's ice crystals that swirl around in the air.

A volcanic tornado forms as Iceland's Fagradalsfjall volcano erupts.

VOLCANIC TORNADOES

A volcano eruption can cause a specific type of tornado, a volcanic tornado. When a volcano explodes, it releases heat into the air. The air then begins to rise and stretch into a column. Sometimes the column begins to spin, making a volcanic tornado. Volcanic tornadoes are made of fire, smoke, and ash. These tornadoes can even pick up lava.

FIRE TORNADOES

Fire tornadoes happen when wildfires combine with tornadoes. Similar to volcanic tornadoes, fire tornadoes happen when warm air rises and transforms into a column. Then the smoky clouds twist into a fire tornado.

A fire tornado in 2020 at the border of California and Nevada

CHAPTER 2:

STRANGE STORMS, LIGHTS, AND ICE

SOME WEATHER EVENTS DON'T NEED TO COMBINE WITH OTHERS TO BE STRANGE. They are weird on their own.

HABOOB

Haboob means "blown" in Arabic. Haboobs, or dust storms, are blowing, dusty walls. They happen when a thunderstorm collapses and pushes out the winds. Then the powerful winds pick up dirt and dust. Haboobs can prevent you from seeing the sun or even a couple of feet in front of you. They can be as wide as 100 miles (161 km) and as tall as 5,000 feet (1,524 m).

A haboob covers the Arizona desert.

CLIMATE CHANGE AND WEIRD WEATHER

While fire tornadoes and other extreme weather events are rare, they are becoming more common with climate change. Climate change is a change in global climate patterns. When people use fossil fuels such as coal and oil, gases are released into the atmosphere and trap heat from the sun. This causes climate change. You can help fight climate change in many ways, such as by buying fewer products, walking and biking when you can, telling government officials you care about the environment, or by joining an environmental group.

LIGHT PILLAR

If you've ever seen a light that looks as though it is shooting up from the ground, you've seen a light pillar. These lights are the easiest to see on humid, windless nights with temperatures below 0°F (−17.8°C). When it is humid, the air has a lot of water in it. Since the temperature is below freezing, the water in the air becomes ice crystals. These crystals in the sky reflect city lights up into the sky.

Light pillars fill the sky on a cold night.

Clouds that are low enough will also be made of ice crystals when light pillars are present.

Icy Clouds

If there are low-level clouds during a light pillar, the cloud will also be made of ice crystals. The clouds can reflect city lights.

HAIR ICE

Sometimes in cold forests, long, white strands hang off rotting branches. They almost look like hair, but they are really ice—hair ice.

It is very rare. To form, it needs wet, rotting wood and humid, cool air. Temperatures must be around 32°F (0°C) to keep its shape. In 2015 scientists found that hair ice also needs fungus. The fungus traps water in the small openings of the wood. Then the water pushes out of the openings. This happens over and over to make hair ice.

Hair ice forming on wood

Nieves penitentes in Chile

NIEVES PENITENTES

Nieves penitentes look like upside-down icicles that stand on the ground. They are made out of snow. They have wide bases and get thinner as they get higher. They can be a couple of inches or even up to 16 feet (4.9 m) tall!

Nieves penitentes form in dry, cool places. They always point toward the sun because they go through sublimation. When they heat up, they don't melt into water. Instead, they turn into water vapor. A smooth layer of snow becomes spiky as some parts of it turn into vapor. Then sunlight hits the lowest parts of the snow, turning it into vapor, making the nieves penitentes even more jagged.

Caspar David Friedrich's 1817 painting "Two Men by the Sea" depicts the ashy skies of the year without a summer.

CHAPTER 3:

REALLY WEIRD WEATHER EVENTS

SOMETIMES THINGS HAPPEN THAT SEEM TOO STRANGE TO HAVE EXISTED. But these weather

THE YEAR WITHOUT A SUMMER

Many people look forward to the sunny, warm days of summer. But those days never arrived for many people around the world in 1816. It is called the year without a summer. The volcano Mount Tambora in Indonesia erupted in 1815. It was the most destructive explosion on Earth in the past ten thousand years. The explosion was so powerful that the volcano's ashes flew into the atmosphere and covered the whole world. The ashes made it hard to see the sun. It also stopped some of the sun's warmth from coming to Earth.

The cool summer came a year later. Temperatures reached record lows. The summer had frost and little sunshine, which kept plants from growing. This meant that many people around the world didn't have enough food.

Mount Tambora is an active volcano in Indonesia that had a powerful explosion in 1815.

BLACK SUNDAY

In the 1930s, dust storms blew across the plains of the US and parts of Canada. Several factors caused the Dust Bowls. The plains were in a severe drought, causing the dirt to dry into dust. Native grasses were ripped up and plowed for farmland. Without the grasses to hold the dirt in place, it blew away.

The Dust Bowl's worst storm is called Black Sunday. Sunday, April 14, 1935, was a bright, sunny day until black dirt blew across the plains. Everything became black. The flying dirt blocked out the sun, and it looked as though it was a dark night. When people went outside, they couldn't see their hand in front of their face. In some areas the dust blew 60 miles (97 km) per hour. While the Black Sunday storm only lasted one day, the Dust Bowl didn't end until about 1939 when it rained enough to hold the soil in the ground.

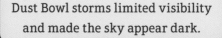

Dust Bowl storms limited visibility and made the sky appear dark.

A dust storm in Rolla, Kansas, in 1935

Blown Away

About 300,000 tons (272,155 t) of topsoil, or the first layer of soil, blew away during Black Sunday. The dust cloud was hundreds of miles wide and thousands of feet high.

TOO HOT TO FLY

Temperatures are becoming more extreme because of climate change. On some extremely hot days, it becomes too hot for planes to fly. Then airlines must delay or cancel flights. This happened in the summer of 2021 in Phoenix, Arizona. When planes take off, they push against the air. The air pushes back, helping lift the plane up. On extremely hot days, the air won't push back on the plane and the plane can't take off.

Pilots can do a few things besides wait for temperatures to drop. Pilots could go faster down the runway. Then the air would push more against the plane. Having longer runways could also work because the planes could take off slowly. Another solution is to lighten the plane so it doesn't have to push as much to fly.

Extremely hot days can make it harder or impossible for planes to take off.

Melting Runway

In 2022 extreme temperatures caused a runway in London, England, to melt. Flights were canceled.

DOUGHNUT-SHAPED HAIL

Typically, hail falls in the shape of a sphere, but in 2021 someone in Wisconsin found hail in the shape of a doughnut. They posted an image of the strange hail online with a ruler showing that it was just a little over an inch (2.5 cm) long. They asked meteorologists what they thought. Meteorologists said that the hail looked as though it had melted. The hail's middle may have been thinner than the rest of it and melted faster, making it look like a doughnut. But the meteorologists were still impressed by the doughnut hail.

Large hail fell during a storm in France in 2022.

Ball lightning is seen in the Netherlands in 2011.

MORE WEIRDNESS

There's more weird weather than what's covered in this book. Blood rain makes it look as though blood is falling from the sky. Red dust combines with the rain, making it red. Strong winds can even push snow to make doughnut-shaped snowballs. Ball lightning is a bright ball of light that can appear during thunderstorms. Scientists are still learning more about these conditions. What weird weather have you seen?

GLOSSARY

atmosphere: the air that surrounds Earth

climate: average weather conditions of a place over a period of years

column: something that is tall and vertical

drought: a long period with little or no rain

electricity: a form of energy with charged particles

erupt: to force out rocks, ash, lava, and more through an explosion

fungus: living things that often look like plants but have no flowers and can't make their own food from sunlight

native: existing, living, or growing originally in a region

sublimation: when a solid directly changes into a vapor

temperature: a measurement to see how hot or cold something is

vapor: something that is in gas form and mixed with the air

LEARN MORE

Ducksters: Dangerous Weather
https://www.ducksters.com/science/dangerous_weather.php

Duling, Kaitlyn. *Hailstorms: Causes and Effects*. Mankato, MN: 12-Story Library, 2022.

Kerry, Isaac. *Climate Change and Extreme Weather*. Minneapolis: Lerner Publications, 2023.

Lewis, Mark L., and Maria Koran. *Storm Rescues*. New York: AV2, 2021.

NASA Climate Kids: Weather and Climate
https://climatekids.nasa.gov/menu/weather-and-climate/

National Geographic Kids: 30 Freaky Facts about the Weather!
https://www.natgeokids.com/uk/discover/geography/physical-geography/30-freaky-facts-about-weather/

Tomecek, Steve. *All about Heat Waves and Droughts*. New York: Children's Press, 2021.

Weather Wiz Kids: Weather Safety
https://www.weatherwizkids.com/weather-safety.htm

INDEX

PHOTO ACKNOWLEDGMENTS

Image credits: Rob Atherton/Shutterstock, pp. 4–5, 9; AP Photo/Jon Pall Vilhelmsson, p. 6–7; Abstract Aerial Art/Digital Vision/Getty Images, p. 10–11; Katelynn & Jordan Hewlett, AP/Wikimedia Commons (CC BY-SA 4.0), p. 12; Stefan Rimaila/Wikimedia Commons (CC BY 3.0), p. 13; John Sirlin/EyeEm/Getty Images, p. 14–15; Christoph Geisler/Wikimedia Commons (CC BY-SA 3.0), p. 17; Timmyjoeelzinga/Wikimedia Commons (CC BY-SA 4.0), p. 18; Vielfalt/Wikimedia Commons (CC BY-SA 4.0), p. 19; ESO/Wikimedia Commons (CC BY 4.0), p. 20; PicturesNow/UIG/Alamy Stock Photo, p. 21; Yus Iran/EyeEm/Getty Images, p. 22–23; Library of Congress Prints and Photographs Division Washington, D.C., p. 24; The U.S. National Archives/Wikimedia Commons PD, p. 25; Nearmap/DigitalVision/Getty Images, p. 26–27; Thierry Zoccolan/AFP/Getty Images, p. 28; Joe Thomissen/Wikimedia Commons (CC BY-SA 3.0), p. 29. Design elements: amgun/Shutterstock.

Cover: Mike Lyvers/Getty Images.